MEET THE ARTIST
Alexandra Franzese

She hand draws all of her coloring books for you guys to enjoy!

She loves chai lattes, cocker spaniels, and spooky season!

Her hometown is Saint Pete, FL. There, she graduated with a BA in Illustration.

She is excited to be able to share her passion for art with you all. Everyday is a joy seeing all of your beautiful finished pages on social media. Use the QR code in the back of this book to follow Alexandra and her artistic journey!

Spooky Mandalas

Alexandra Franzese

Spooky Mandalas by: Alexandra Franzese

Spooky Mandalas by: Alexandra Franzese

Spooky Mandalas by: Alexandra Franzese

Spooky Mandalas by: Alexandra Franzese

Spooky Mandalas by: Alexandra Franzese

Spooky Mandalas by: Alexandra Franzese

Spooky Mandalas by: Alexandra Franzese

Spooky Mandalas by: Alexandra Franzese

Spooky Mandalas by: Alexandra Franzese

Spooky Mandalas by: Alexandra Franzese

Spooky Mandalas by: Alexandra Franzese

Spooky Mandalas by: Alexandra Franzese

Spooky Mandalas by: Alexandra Franzese

Spooky Mandalas by: Alexandra Franzese

Spooky Mandalas by: Alexandra Franzese

Spooky Mandalas by: Alexandra Franzese

Spooky Mandalas by: Alexandra Franzese

Spooky Mandalas by: Alexandra Franzese

Spooky Mandalas by: Alexandra Franzese

Spooky Mandalas by: Alexandra Franzese

Spooky Mandalas by: Alexandra Franzese

Spooky Mandalas by: Alexandra Franzese

Spooky Mandalas by: Alexandra Franzese

Spooky Mandalas by: Alexandra Franzese

Spooky Mandalas by: Alexandra Franzese

Spooky Mandalas by: Alexandra Franzese

Spooky Mandalas by: Alexandra Franzese

Spooky Mandalas by: Alexandra Franzese

Spooky Mandalas by: Alexandra Franzese

Spooky Mandalas by: Alexandra Franzese

Spooky Mandalas by: Alexandra Franzese

Spooky Mandalas by: Alexandra Franzese

Spooky Mandalas by: Alexandra Franzese

Spooky Mandalas by: Alexandra Franzese

Spooky Mandalas by: Alexandra Franzese

Spooky Mandalas by: Alexandra Franzese

Spooky Mandalas by: Alexandra Franzese

Spooky Mandalas by: Alexandra Franzese

Spooky Mandalas by: Alexandra Franzese

Spooky Mandalas by: Alexandra Franzese

Spooky Mandalas by: Alexandra Franzese

Spooky Mandalas by: Alexandra Franzese

Spooky Mandalas by: Alexandra Franzese

Spooky Mandalas by: Alexandra Franzese

Spooky Mandalas by: Alexandra Franzese

Spooky Mandalas by: Alexandra Franzese

Spooky Mandalas by: Alexandra Franzese

Spooky Mandalas by: Alexandra Franzese

Spooky Mandalas by: Alexandra Franzese

Spooky Mandalas by: Alexandra Franzese

Spooky Mandalas by: Alexandra Franzese

Spooky Mandalas by: Alexandra Franzese

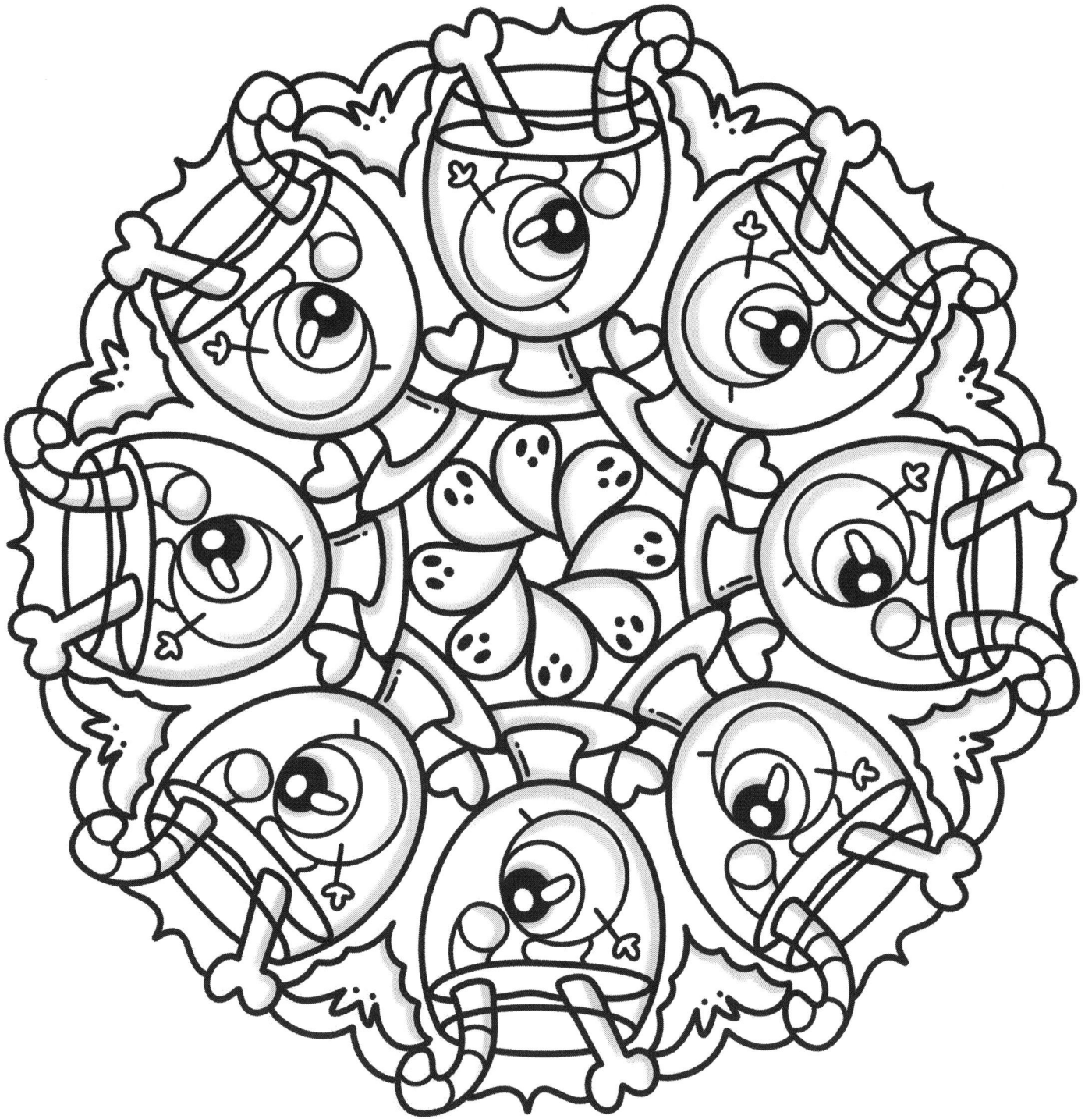

BONUS PAGE

Fall Mandalas by:
Alexandra Franzese

Get your next book

Spooky Mandalas by: Alexandra Franzese

Scan Me!

Scan for: More books, Etsy shops, Social Links

Thank You for Your Support!

By purchasing my books you are supporting an independent artist.

Remember to leave an Amazon review of any purchased book

Post colored pages!

Post your pages in our **facebook group** and tag me on **instagram** and **TikTok!** #alexandrafranzese

Subscribe to my emails to get a FREE coloring page once a month!

Get featured in my insta Stories!

New books are released once a month!
follow me for updates

Travel Size Books Available!

FB group: Coloring Books by Alexandra Franzese and Joshua Dunbar

Made in the USA
Las Vegas, NV
07 September 2024